HOW TO ENTERTAIN YOUR GUESTS

HOW TO
ENTERTAIN
YOUR
GUESTS

A BOOK OF INDOOR GAMES

Collected by
Dorothy Dickinson

Copper Beech Publishing

Published in Great Britain by
Copper Beech Publishing Ltd
This edition © Copper Beech Publishing Ltd 1993

ISBN 0 9516295 4 9
A CIP catalogue record for this book is available from
The British Library.

Cover photograph and some illustrations
taken from 'The Queen' - The Ladies Newspaper.
Reproduced by kind permission of The National
Magazine Company. Coin photographs reproduced with
permission of The Royal Mint.
Other illustrations reproduced with permission
from private collections.

Copper Beech Gift Books
Copper Beech Publishing Ltd
PO Box 159 East Grinstead
Sussex England RH19 4FS

TO ALL THE
HOSTS AND HOSTESSES OF
MEN WOMEN AND CHILDREN
WHO
AT ONE TIME OR ANOTHER
HAVE NOT KNOWN WHAT
TO DO WITH THEIR GUESTS,
THIS BOOK IS
SYMPATHETICALLY DEDICATED.

PREFACE

That no apology for the appearance of this collection of games is necessary can be taken for granted when one recollects the vast number of hosts and hostesses who do not know what to do with their guests when they have got them, and when one remembers the long evenings which have passed so slowly because no one has had courage enough to propose a new game or foresight enough to come prepared with a mental list of games that "go".

The object of this volume is to try to lessen the number of dreadful pauses by bringing together some of the games that we have found by our own experience to go with a right good swing. A hundred or so of such will be sufficient to form a good background for working purposes, and if the hostess will but look them through beforehand, and thus meet her guests prepared for their entertainment in that direction as well as in others, she need have no fear of her parties not going off well. The only hostesses for whom it is not safe to do this are those who do not want their friends to enjoy themselves and to wish to come again.

Those games we have called 'Competitions' need preparing before the arrival of the visitors, as they cannot be rushed at the last minute. It is as well to decide before sending out the invitations what is to be the piece de resistance, and then to write it on the top of the invitation card. 'An Evening With Kate', 'Violets', will serve to arouse the curiosity of those who do not know the games, and make them all the more anxious to come to find out what the new form of entertainment is. A little forethought goes a very long way, and parties thus prepared for will be remembered for ages as some of the most enjoyable possible.

Perhaps some of those who purchase this collection will be disappointed when they find that they know most of the games contained therein. If they do know them, well and good: so much the better for their visitors; but have they been able always to remember them at the crucial moment? Have they ever felt that they could not think of another to save their lives, even though there was a very great danger of their party being flat? If they have, then we hope that, by glancing through this collection beforehand, the feeling will be banished for ever. If this book helps any of them out of such difficulties, then our time and our trouble will not have been wasted.

That some of our readers know many of the games contained herein we readily believe, but there are others who are not so fortunate. We had doubts, for instance, about the advisability of 'Clumps', until a few days ago, when we happened to be present at a gathering of maidens and youths whose ages varied from seventeen to twenty-seven or so. The inevitable question was asked in due time "What shall we do now?" - and when we ventured mildly to suggest 'Clumps' we were considerably surprised to find that not a single other person in the room knew how to play it. Wherefore we refuse to apologise for the existence of this book.

One word of advice more. It is a good plan to have one of the 'Competitions' arranged for the first part of the evening. Most of the games in this section will make the guests move about the room, and so come into contact with others whom they may not have met before. The ball is set rolling in this way, and only the very shyest visitor is proof against such an introduction. After this first game is ended, then go on with one of the livelier ones, and by the time that is finished the hostess will find that everything is working together for good, and that her visitors will go away when the time comes, feeling that they have had a right royal time, and wondering when she will ask them to come again. In fact, she need not be surprised if they refuse definitely to go at the specified time, but persist in staying for another hour or so.

Finally, we would offer our best thanks to all who have, consciously or unconsciously, helped us in making this collection. Perhaps if this one is kindly received by our readers, a fresh volume may follow in due course. We hope so, but it rests entirely with them.

D.D.

COMPETITIONS

For winning the games in this section, the hostess may give some small present as a prize. This is by no means absolutely necessary, though it adds to the interest of the game. Or, if she prefers, she can arrange for two or three of the games to be played during the same evening, and give one prize for the best combined results.

This works very well, as it gives a chance to those who may not be quick at one game, but who can do well at another.

No 1
AN EVENING WITH KATE

The guests on arrival are provided with pencils and cards on which are twenty-four ruled and numbered lines. About the room are hung sheets of paper on which the players must find among words ending with the syllable '-cate'. It is better to have half-a-dozen sheets with four or five questions on each, rather than all the questions on one sheet, as the guests will thus have to move about and mix with one another. At the end of a given time, say twenty minutes, the cards are corrected, and prizes can be awarded to the most successful.

Below are a few questions and answers to show how it could be arranged.

Questions	Answers
To inscribe to anyone	Dedicate
To train	Educate
To foretell	Prognosticate
To oil	Lubricate
To recommend	Advocate
To rub out	Eradicate

As many as are thought to be necessary can be found easily in any dictionary; but, to save the time of the hostess, we give a few, for which questions can be made without difficulty: Abdicate, Collocate, Communicate, Complicate, Confiscate, Duplicate, Defalcate, Deprecate, Embrocate, Fabricate, Implicate, Imprecate, Indicate, Inculcate, Judicate, Locate, Masticate, Medicate, Placate, Pontificate, Predicate, Vacate, Vindicate.

No 2
ROSEBUDS

In this game the players have to find the answers to the questions, or, more accurately, the words suggested and referred to by the short sentences, which are written out on sheets of paper or thin cardboard and hung about the room. All the letters of each of these words referred to are to be found in the one word 'ROSEBUDS'. All questions are based on the same idea, and a specimen question is:

"What old maids sometimes are, milk often is, and vinegar always is, and the answer "Sour", the letters S,O,U,R, all occurring in the word 'Rosebuds'.

The question papers are to be hung about the room where they can be seen by every one, not all together or near each other, but scattered if possible, so that the players will have to move about and mix, and in that way get to know each other a little more. The cards on which the answers are to be written should have been prepared beforehand, and should have as many lines numbered and ruled on them as there are questions to be answered. These are then distributed, and the players told what to do. For this they are allowed half-an-hour, or more if they ask for it, after which they must stop writing, and the answers are read out. To the one who has the most answers right, a small prize can be given.

If the hostess wishes, she can present to each of her guests on arrival a rosebud, or a bowl of roses may form the basis of the flower decoration of the room. A little care in arranging details such as these will add immensely to the enjoyment of the evening. Or if she prefers, a bunch of roses can be given as the prize. There are many ways in which the game will suggest the making use of the flower, all of which ensure and increase the success of the party.

The principal reason why gatherings at which this and kindred games form the *piece de resistance* are successful, is that the guests are bound to come in contact with each other, and it is only natural for them to become on friendly terms for the rest of the evening, and so pass the time all the more pleasantly - which is what every hostess wishes.

Here we offer a list of questions and answers, which may be taken as specimens if the hostess prefers to work out her own set.

1. A county in Scotland-*Ross*
2. A means of progression nearly as slow as a well-known Southern railway service-*Bus*
3. A slang word meaning to sleep-*Doss*
4. What all anglers like to hold-*Rod*
5. The prickly head of a plant-*Bur*
6. What washerwomen like to have when washing-*Suds*
7. A girl's name-*Bess*
8. The state in which every one prefers a man to be-*Sober*
9. A part of every well-ordered garden-*Sod*
10. A people who have lately become our friends-*Boers*
11. A colour we sometimes see in the sky-*Red*
12. To pour water on any one or anything-*Douse*
13. What we have to do to clothes to wash them-*Rub*
14. A state of mind in which some people are without sufficient cause-*Sure*
15. A word that signifies worthless matter-Dross

16. What mothers wish to see on the faces of their children-*Roses*

17. A word meaning to confer a title on any one-*Dub*

18 A state of mind impossible for those playing this game-*Bored*

19. Part of a fish eaten as a delicacy-*Roe*

20. A long gown-*Robe*

21. A round and usually solid body-*Orb*

22. A damaged part of the body-Sore

23. An action which, when done by a woman always upsets a man-*Sobs*

24. A flower in an early stage-*Bud*

25. A slang name for a master-*Boss*

26. What ladies like to do in the latest fashion-*Dress*

27. A word meaning 'impolite'-*Rude*

28. A trick done to deceive others-*Ruse*

29. To stir up others to action-*Rouse*

30. That to which we go with reluctance and we leave with displeasure-*Bed*

Other words are: Rose, Rob, Rode, Or, Bore, Bode, Dour, Do, Use, Doer.

No 3
GUESSING SHADOWS

The best place to play this is an a room where there is a bay window or an alcove, though a corner of the room will do if the others are wanting. Across the front of the window is tied a string from which hang all sorts of articles-say for example, a corkscrew, a knife, a cigar, a cream jug, a potato, a carrot etc – a few inches apart. Then hang a white sheet in front of them to hide them from the view of the players, and light one or two lamps or candles behind, so that the shadows of the articles can be clearly seen on the sheet. It is necessary to number the places on the sheet where the shadows fall so that the players can record their guesses on cards or paper provided beforehand, ready numbered, for the purpose. The lights in the room are then lowered, and the lamps behind turned up, and the players allowed a quarter of an hour to guess. Of course, they must not touch the sheet. At the end of that time the correct list is read out, and the one who has the greatest number right is declared the winner.

No 4
A NOAH'S ARK PARTY

The invitations are sent out with 'NOAH'S ARK' printed in the corner.

To each guest on arrival a pencil and numbered card are given and on the back of the card the name of an animal is written *e.g.* donkey, cat, elephant, the same name being written on two cards only, one of which is given to a lady and the other to a gentleman, the owners of these two cards eventually going in to supper together. In front of the card leave a blank line with the words 'Sketched by' above it.

Each guest must then draw as well as he or she is able, the animal named on the back of the card and after ten or fifteen minutes these are collected and arranged round the room. Every one is then given another card on which to write down, on the numbered lines left for that purpose, the names of the animals they think the various sketches are supposed to represent, the sketch-cards being already numbered by the hostess before distribution. The name is signed at the foot of the guessing-card, and the one who has guessed the greatest number correctly is awarded a prize.

Two judges may then examine the drawings and award

another prize to the most successful artist.

The competition may last from an hour to an hour and a half, and always proves most amusing.

No 5

THE FLOWER WEDDING
A game to 'break the ice'

This is a very good game for making things 'go' during the first thirty or forty minutes and getting guests to mix, and so break the ice, which frequently does not thaw till it is nearly time for the party to break up.

The questions are written clearly – or printed – on large sheets of paper or thin cardboard, and the sheets are hung about the room, – four or five questions on each sheet. It is better to have several sheets than one large one, as the moving from one to the other which is necessary makes it easier for the guests to mix and get to know each other. The visitors are provided with pencils and cards (correspondence cards answer very well for this), on which are ruled and numbered thirty lines, between which and opposite the corresponding numbers, the answers are to be written. The questions refer to a wedding, and the answers are to be found among the names of flowers. Half-an-hour is allowed for the guessing, after which the correct answers are read out and the cards marked.

To the one who has succeeded in making the most answers correctly, the hostess can give a small prize. Those who have not tried the game before will be surprised when they find with what favour it is received.

The following thirty questions and answers are specimens and others can be made up if desired.

1. What was his rank and surname? – *Marechal Neil*
2. What was his disposition and Christian name? – *Sweet William*
3. What was one of the bridegroom's qualities? – *Thrift*
4. What was his motive in marrying her? – *Marigold*
5. Where did she live and what was her appearance? – *Canterbury Bell*
6. How far did he come to see her? – *Camomile*
7. What did he say at parting? – *Forget-me-not*
8. What did she say when they parted? – *Speedwell*

9. What was she at her first ball? – *Wallflower*

10. What did he wear the last time before he was married?
– *Bachelor's Buttons*

11. What was the name of the best man? – *William Allan Richardson*

12. What was the name of the clergyman? – *Jonquil*

13. What was the colour of her going-away dress? – *Heliotrope*

14. What did they throw after the carriage? – *Lady's Slipper*

15. What did the wedding cause in the town? – *Aster* (A stir)

16. How many went to the wedding? – *Phlox*

17. What did the guests wear to the wedding? – *Furze*

18. What were used to decorate the town? – *Flags*

19. What did he say his love for her was? - *Everlasting*

20. What was one of the presents? – *Broom*

21. Where was his money made? – *Mint*

22. In what was his money invested? – *Stocks*

23. What did the guests do when the wedding march was played? – *Rose*

24. Of what were the sweets made? – *Cornflower*

25. What kind of cigarettes did he smoke? – *Woodbine*

26. What kind of pipes did he smoke? – *Briar*

27. What did she feed him on? – *Oxlips*

28. What was one of her good qualities? - *Honesty*

29. What was the ginger-beer like at the wedding breakfast? - *Poppy*

30. How much tea did the bride take? - *Buttercup*

If the hostess be able to paint or draw, she can illustrate the sheets of questions with paintings of flowers. This adds greatly to the general effect produced.

No 6
FLORIN COMPETITION

Each competitor is provided with a two-shilling piece which has been issued in Queen Victoria's reign since the beginning of the year 1896, and a numbered card on which to write the answers to the questions, all of which answers are to be found on the florin.

The questions can be written on sheets of paper and hung about the room, and twenty minutes or so be allowed for the answering, after which the cards are corrected, and prizes given to the most successful. Here are some sample questions, all of which, with or without additional ones, may be used.

A peculiarity of Chester – *Rose (Rows)*
A Queen's Mother-in-law – *Queen Victoria*
A door fastener – *Chain*
A coin of greater value – *Crown*
Between two hills – *Veil (Vale)*
A Biblical animal's food – *Thistle*
An English Port – *Shields*
A moorland plant – *Shamrock*
Coins of lesser value – *Pense (Pence)*
A timid animal – *Hair (Hare)*
Another name for Pitch and Toss – *Heads and Tails*
In the midst of sin and crime – *The letter I*
A black fiend – *Imp*
A French town – *Lions (Lyons)*
A newspaper – *Star*
A spirit – *Gin (in the word Regina)*
Symbolical of sweetness – *Honi (Honey)*

No 7
PROGRESSIVE GAME

This is an excellent and popular way of spending a good part of the evening. Care should be taken to get an even number of players and, if possible, half of them ladies and half gentlemen. A different game is needed for each four players and most of the well-known games are suitable, such as Draughts, Whist, and games with dice, as, for instance, Racing Games, where a special board and little lead horses or ships are provided. Other games may be arranged at some of the other tables. At one there may be a large bowl half-full of hard, dry peas, which the players have to spear with previously-blunted hatpins, one hatpin to each player. At a second table may be another bowl, filled with small beans, which have to be taken out with two lead pencils, which must be held in one hand only. At another there may be four wine-glasses and four large boxes of matches (containing an equal number of matches) the players having with two of the matches to place all the matches on the top (*i.e.* resting on the rim) of the glasses in the given time.

For twenty players it is necessary to have five tables which may be distributed thus; No 1, The Peas; No 2, The Race-Game; No 3, Draughts; No 4, The Beans; No 5, The Matches. In the Draughts game it is advisable to play the quick game, each trying to lose as many as possible. Should more than five tables be required, the others can be made up of almost any children's game - Snap, Beggar-my-neighbour, or a game like the Fishpond which, however, will have to be bought at a shop. It is quite easy to provide a good evening's entertainment for very little cost.

It is necessary to have score-cards on which the players can record the number of games won, so that a small prize can be given at the end of the most successful one. Badges, such as are used at progressive whist parties, and which can be obtained at any stationer's, should be given to the guests on arrival, this being a simple method of settling which lady is to play with which gentleman, the gentlemen's cards being numbered to indicate the table at which they are to commence playing.

When the guests have assembled and sorted themselves out, explain to them exactly what is expected at each table. They are not to start before the signal, and they are to stop as soon as the bell rings. Then the two winners (the two who have got the most peas or beans out, for instance) are to put a W on their score-cards, the others putting the letter L. The two winners then move on to the next table, the gentleman sitting opposite the lady he finds there and the lady opposite the gentleman. The losers stay at the same table till they can win. Not more than four minutes should be allowed for each game.

The game lasts for twenty or twenty-four rounds, after which the points are counted and the prizes distributed.

No 8
HOLE IN THE SHEET

A sheet is hung in the doorway of the room and in it a hole about the size of half-a-crown is cut. The players are divided into sides, one side staying in the room, the other going out. The members of the retiring side in turn place one of their eyes at the hole, and it is the duty of the members inside the room to guess to whom the eye belongs. The eye remains at the hole for only a very short time, and then, after holding a consultation (which to the outsiders is often very amusing) the captain calls out the name of the alleged owner of the eye. If it is right, one point is counted to them; if wrong, to the other side.

It is better, if possible, for the inside of the room to be well lighted, and the outside in semi-darkness, or the shadows of those outside may betray them.

No 9
HANDS AND FEET GUESSING

The players are divided into two sides, one going out of the room, the other staying in. In front of the open door place a screen, above which no players of the opposite side can be seen. Those who are on the outside then walk past, holding their hands above the top of the screen. Those left in the room must then guess whose hand it is, and if right they score a point. After all of A's side have shown a hand, B's side goes out, and does the same. The players who score the most points in the end, win.

If the feet are to be shown instead of the hands, the screen should be raised not more than a few inches from the floor, so that just the shoes may be seen underneath, the game then proceeding as above.

No 10
THE LABYRINTH

An inexpensive present will be required for each guest invited. These presents are fastened to the end of long ribbons of different colours, which are twisted in and out among trees and shrubs and with the other ribbons until they are in a tangle, while the end to which the present is fastened is laid under a bush or plant, the other ends all being brought to one place, a grass plot preferably and laid in a row.

Each guest on arrival is given one ribbon and told to unravel it and find at the end a reward for his labour; or, if the hostess wishes to give a further small present, all may be started at once and the one reaching the end first receive the extra gift.

If ribbon is too expensive, tape or even string may be used instead; and if there is no garden handy, the room, if large enough, or hall, will do.

No 11
DO YOU KNOW HIM?

This is another of those games which help the visitors to pass an enjoyable half-hour, and for which, if the hostess wish, a small prize may be given.

A number of picture postcards of celebrities are stuck about the room, each numbered, but with the name of the person hidden. The competitors are given pencils and papers containing numbers corresponding to those on the photographs. They are then asked to write opposite each number the name of the original of each portrait.

A judicious mixture of photographs, of which there should be at least two dozen, will provide a very good half-hour's amusement, suitable for players of all ages. The list should contain amongst others, statesmen, churchmen, actors and actresses, sportsmen, local celebrities, musicians, writers etc. These can be varied, if thought desi by having pictures of differen places in England and abroad

No 12
BABY PHOTOGRAPHS

This is a very good way of entertaining one's guests

Cards of invitation are sent out with the words 'BABY PARTY' printed in the corner, and each visitor is requested to bring with him or her one of his photographs taken when a child. These are handed in to the hostess on arrival, and she marks or numbers them or arranges them about the room. The guests are then given pencils and papers already numbered, and asked to guess whose photographs

they are. A small prize may be given to the one who has the greatest number of correct answers.

No 13
THE BIRDS' WEDDING

This is a game similar to the Flower Wedding though of course with a different set of questions and answers.

The questions are written on sheets of paper, which are hung around the room so that the competitors have to mix with each other in going from one paper to another. Four or five questions should be on each paper. Players have to write down what they think to be correct answers on cards prepared for this purpose. Of course, they should not consult each other during the time allowed for guessing. At the end of about half-an-hour, "Time" is called, and the correct answers are read out, the one with the highest number of correct answers is proclaimed the winner, and receiving whatever small prize the hostess wishes to give.

The following are the questions and answers:-

1. Who was the bridegroom? - *Albatross*
2. Who was the bride? - *Kittywake*
3. Who was the best man? - *Jackdaw*
4. Who was the bridesmaid? - *Jenny Wren*
5. Who married them? - *Pastor Bird*
6. Who made the bride's trousseau? - *Jay*
7. Who made the bridegroom's clothes? - *Tailor-bird*
8. What did the bridegroom wear on his head? - *Black Cap*
9. Who made the wedding cake? - *Buzzard*
10. What did they drink? - *Canary*
11. Who wore the darkest clothes? - *Black-bird*
12. Why did they all go to church on bicycles? - For a *Lark*

13. What make of machines did they use? – *Swift*

14. How did the stout relation arrive? – *Puffin*

15. What royalty was present? – *Kingfisher*

16. From where did the most distant guest come? – *Turkey*

17. Who wore the grandest dress? – *Peacock*

18. What did the bridegroom make of his fortune? – *Ducks and Drakes*

19. What was one of the guests caught doing? – *Robin (!)*

20. What kind of a ring did the bridegroom wear? – *Cygnet*

21. Who wore a paper tail? – *Kite*

22. Who provided the music? – *Humming-bird*

23. Who brought his own musical instrument? – *Lyre*

24. Who lifted the luggage into the carriage? – *Crane*

25. With what was the house decorated? – *Bunting*

26. Who made the silliest joke? – *Goose*

27. Who nailed up the decorations? – *Yellowhammer*

28. Who provided a delicacy for the breakfast? – *Oyster-catcher*

29. With what pen was the contract signed? – *Swan*

30. Who acknowledged the presents? – *Secretary-bird*

31. What kind of guests were there? – *Divers*

32. What did the bride wear round her neck? – *Ruff*

33. What did she put in her hair? – *Osprey*

34. What did the cat do? – *Emu!!!*

No 14
PICTURE GUESSING

Twenty or thirty copies of well-known pictures are hung about the room after all marks of identification (such as names etc) have been covered over. These copies can easily be secured at small cost in the shape of cheap reprints or pictures cut out of the illustrated magazines or may be borrowed from postcard albums. So long as the picture is fairly clear, size matters little. Players are asked to write the correct name of each picture on cards provided for the purpose, on which are numbers corresponding to those attached to the pictures. For this they are allowed twenty minutes or so, or if it be a 'Social Evening', and there are other games and methods of entertainment to pass the time, a longer period may be given. At the end of the time, all must stop writing, and cards are collected and marked. The one with the most answers right is declared the winner.

It may be advisable for the hostess, who is contemplating having this competition in the future, to keep her eyes open for reproductions, to secure them whenever she comes across them, and keep them by her. A little foresight will save a lot of worry as the time gets shorter and she has to busy herself in other directions.

No 15
GUESSING WEIGHTS

A splendid game!

This is a recommended game for grown-ups as well as for those a little younger. A tray, on which are placed several different articles, which have been previously weighed and the weights noted, is brought into the room and those present, who are provided with paper and pencil, are asked to write down what they think the various things weigh. The competitor who guesses the most correct weight of the greatest number of things wins the small prize which may be awarded. The following articles are suggested as examples: a shoe, a pincushion, a tea-cup and saucer, a stone, a small box, a poker. The hostess can add as many more as she thinks desirable.

A variety of this game can be played by putting different articles not only to be weighed but also to be measured, etc. For instance, there might be a stone to be weighed, a ball of string the length of which has to be guessed, the number of matches contained in a box, and so on.

No 16
WHO AM I?

For this game it is better to have made preparations before the guests arrive. On separate slips of paper are written the names of different celebrities, such as Oliver Cromwell, Robespierre, Macbeth, Shylock, Pickwick, Robin Hood, The Prince of Wales, and the like; one of these slips is then pinned on to the back of each of the players, whose duty it is to discover the name written by asking questions of any of the other players who will answer, no one being allowed to ask two questions from the same player. Take 'Cromwell' as an example, and you will get some such conversation as this:-

Q. Am I alive?

A. No

Q. Did I live last century?

A. No

Q. In the 17th century?

A. Yes

Q. Was I a politician?

A. Yes

..... and so on.

Of course, it is necessary to have a good reserve supply of slips, for as soon as the questioner guesses one name he must take the paper from his back and pin it to his coat in front, asking the hostess to give him another for his back; the one who guesses the most in a given time being declared the winner.

No 17
ANAGRAMS
A good way of spending the first part of an evening

The hostess must prepare beforehand a sufficient number of slips of paper, on which are written words, all the letters of which are out of place. Thus, if one of the words chosen be 'NOISY', the letters on the paper might be written 'YINSO' or in any way the hostess wishes. One of these numbered slips, each containing a different word, is then pinned on the coat or blouse of each guest, who receives also a card with numbered spaces, corresponding to the numbers on the slips, and a pencil. The visitors then go round and puzzle out what each combination of letters represents, and put the answer thus arrived at on the cards opposite the right numbers. The one who guesses the greatest number correct wins the prize, if there be one.

No 18
BOOK TEAS

Some hostesses may not care to have their guests for the whole evening, but may prefer to have them for an hour or two in the afternoon. For such, 'Book Teas' are popular for helping to pass the time. At the top left-hand corner of the cards of invitation 'BOOK TEA' is written, so that each visitor arrives with an illustration of some Book Title. The illustration may be humorous or otherwise, according to

the taste of the guest. On arrival, each guest is given a pencil and numbered card, on which to write the title of the book represented by each of the other guests. It will be simplest if the answer is put down opposite the name of each guest (previously written by the hostess on the card), in the fol-

lowing manner:-

> Mrs Brown   *The Heavenly Twins*
> Mrs Jones   *The Lilac Sunbonnet*
> Mrs Smith   *The Ring and the Book*

The one wins who has the fullest list of correct answers at the end.

No 19
CATHEDRAL TOWN TEAS

Like most of the games in this section, this may be used for an afternoon tea-party or for part of a whole evening's entertainment. The guests are asked to come provided with some illustration of a Cathedral Town, or of a Cathedral itself pinned on to their dresses or coats in a conspicuous place. The name of the Town or Cathedral, as the case may be, must of course be covered up beforehand by the guests. The hostess must have prepared cards, as in the previous competition, by writing the names of her visitors, in alphabetical order, down the left-hand side, and ruling a line across the card under each name. Correspondence cards will do very well. These cards are then handed to the guests, who are asked to write down the name of the Cathedral, or Town. To the one who gets the most answers right, she can give some small present as a reward.

No 20
NURSERY RHYMES

Cards are hung about the room with a short description of nursery rhymes or characters written thereon. The guests are provided with cards already ruled and numbered from 1 to 24, in which spaces they are to write the names of the rhymes described. To the one who gets the most right a small prize may be given, should the hostess wish.

The descriptions and answers below are suggestions, and have already proved useful and entertaining where they have been tried.

1. One who was too previous – *The Man in the Moon*

2. One who took a journey to see Royalty – *Pussy Cat, Pussy Cat, where have you been?*

3. One who practised horticulture with astonishing results – *Mary, Mary, quite contrary*

4. One who, at the festive season, exhibited an unwarrantable pride in his own virtues – *Little Jack Horner*

5. A proposal, and a reason why it should be accepted – *Curly-locks, Curly-locks*

6. A triumph of the culinary art – *Sing a song of sixpence*

7. Shows that musicians are born, not made – *Tom, Tom, the Piper's Son*

8. One who was lazy and neglected the call of duty - *Little Boy Blue*

9. A peregrinating bird - *Goosey, Goosey, Gander*

10. One of a nervous temperament who, while partaking of some light refreshment, was rudely interrupted - *Little Miss Muffet*

11. One who unaccountably lost sight of her belongings, and advice as to the return thereof - *Little Bo Peep*

12. A genial old gentleman, with decidedly musical taste - *Old King Cole*

13. A variety of taste, with no waste - *Jack Sprat*

14. A sad tale of poverty, and a kind-hearted old soul - *Old Mother Hubbard*

15. A subject worthy of the notice of the R.S.P.C.A. - *Ding Dong Bell, Pussy's in the well.*

16. A sad climbing fatality - *Jack and Jill*

17. An historic fight, ending in the defeat of an extinct animal - *The Lion and the Unicorn*

18. A journey to town to see a much decorated lady, accompanied by music - *Ride-a-cock-horse*

19. Him what takes what isn't hisn, when he's kotched gets sent to prison - *The Queen of Hearts, she made some tarts*

20. The story of a young lady, who only got as much as she worked for - *See-Saw, Margery Daw*

ROUND GAMES

How many words a minute?
Scandal Whispering
Passing Pennies
Shadows - Picking up Potatoes
Missing Adjectives - Blowing the Feather
Throwing cards into a hat
How? Why? Where?
Obstacle Race
How do you like your Neighbours?
Throwing the Handkerchief - I Shine
Clumps - Charades - Dumb Crambo
Miew - Stool of Repentance
Family Coach
Pinning on the Donkey's Tail

No 21
HOW MANY WORDS A MINUTE

Sides are chosen, and a time-keeper and a scorer appointed. A player from A's party then goes out of the room, while B's party decides on a letter. He is then called in again, the time-keeper says "Go", the letter is told him, and he has to say as fast as he can as many English words beginning with that letter as he can remember, the scorer counting one point for each word. At the end of a minute, "Time" is called, and he must stop, and his score is counted and read out. One of B's side then goes through the same ordeal, and so on alternately, till all the players have had their turns. The scores of each side are then added up, the one with the largest score winning. Any letter may be chosen except X and Z.

No 22
SCANDAL

This is quite a good game to cause fun and laughter.

One of the party goes out of the room while all the others make remarks about him, which are put down on paper by the scandal monger. When every one has said something, complimentary or otherwise, about him, the victim is called back into the room, and the scandal-monger begins to read out from his list; "Some one says you are very lazy" and the unfortunate one has to guess who the some-one is.

If he can guess right, that one must take his turn and go out and be talked about. If he does not guess, they can be re-read, or either he must go out again, or one of the others must volunteer.

No 23
WHISPERING

The company is seated round the room, and one starts the telegram by whispering a sentence of some kind to his neighbour, who then whispers what he heard, or thought he heard, to his neighbour, and so on round the room, on no account repeating his message, even though the recipient declares he has not heard a word. When the message has gone round the room, the last to receive it must repeat it aloud as he heard it, the originator then giving the original message. The two are not usually alike, and great fun can be had in noting the difference between them.

No 24
PASSING PENNIES

The players sit in two rows, an equal number in each, with A sitting at the top between the two end players, and B at the bottom in a similar position. A holds two pennies, one in each hand, which he drops at the same moment, one into the left hand of his right-hand neighbour, and the other into the right hand of his left-hand neighbour. These two then pass on

their pennies to their neighbours, the one on the right putting it into the left hand of the one next to him, and the other into the right hand of the one next to him. No 2 then passes it on to No 3 and so on till it comes to the end one in each row who has to touch B's hand with his penny and then pass it back again to A as quickly as possible, this time the players using their other hands. As soon as it reaches No 1 he puts it into A's waiting hand, and the side whose penny is safely deposited with A the first, scores the point.

Thirteen points make the game.

No 25
SHADOWS

A sheet is hung up in a doorway so as to cover all the open space. The players are divided into two sides, one side remains in the room, the other goes out into the passage. The lights in the room are then lowered, while a lamp giving a strong light is placed on a high table in the passage, so as to be on a level with the average player's head. Those in the passage then walk between the light and the sheet, remaining there for twenty or thirty seconds so that the profile shadows of their heads are thrown on to the sheet. The other side must guess whose shadow they see. When all have passed by, they change places. The side making the greater number of correct guesses wins the game.

No 26
PICKING UP POTATOES

This is another game in which sides of equal numbers are necessary. On the floor are arranged eight potatoes in two rows of four each, at equal distances from a tray which stands at the head of each row, a couple of feet beyond the nearest potato. Two players, one from each side, then try to pick up the potatoes with salt-spoons and place them safely in the trays. No help may be given at all, either by the hand, foot, or another piece of furniture. Both stop as soon as the first has put his four in his tray, when he is credited with four points, and his opponent with as many as he has potatoes in his tray. After each player in his turn has tried, the potatoes are exchanged, and the players try again with the other set of potatoes, the side whose total is the largest in the end winning the game.

No 27
MISSING ADJECTIVES

This is a game which can be prepared in about five minutes. Take a paragraph from ten to fifteen lines in length from some interesting or amusing book and make a list of all the adjectives used, marking them in the book so that they can be easily seen.

Provide all the players with pencils and paper, and read out the selected lines, leaving a blank space where each adjective comes. When they have copied this down, read out the list of adjectives, and tell them to put them into their proper places. Of course, care should be taken not to read out the words in their correct order! Five minutes are allowed, and then the results are read out.

BLOWING THE FEATHER

No 28
BLOWING THE FEATHER

This is a game to enliven things, and can be played in two slightly different ways.

1. A large sheet is held by those who are playing, who stand round the outside. A feather is thrown into the middle of the sheet, and each tries to blow it to the opposite one. If there is no sheet handy, the players can sit round the table.

2. Instead of standing round a sheet, the players sit in two rows facing each other. A line is drawn on the floor from one end to the other midway between the rows and for this string will do, if it is fastened tight enough. The feather is then blown upwards, and each side must try to make the feather fall on the opposite side of the line, and every time they succeed in doing this a point is scored, whereas if the feather drops on their side of the line the point is scored by their opponents. The side which first scores thirteen points in this way wins the game.

Toy balloons may be used instead of feathers if desired, but a reserve stock should be handy.

No 29
THROWING CARDS INTO A HAT

The players are divided into two sides, each side sitting in a semi-circle so that each member may be an equal distance from the top-hat or bowl, which is placed in the centre of the room. Each side is then provided with a pack of playing cards (with different coloured backs, to facilitate the counting at the end), which are divided up so that each player has six cards.

The end member of A's side then tries to throw his cards, one at a time, into the hat. He is followed by one of B's side, and so on, alternately, till all have tried. The cards are then taken out of the hat and counted, a record being kept till the end of the game. At the second round the players throw two cards at a time, at the third three, and at the fourth all the six. The points thus scored are all added up at the end of the game, the side with the larger total winning the game.

No 30
HOW? WHEN? WHERE?

One of the players goes out of the room, while the others choose a certain word or object. The guesser must find out what the word or object is by asking each in turn the question *"How did you like it?"*

If he has not guessed by the end of the first round of questionings, he starts again with
"When do you like it?"

If a third round is necessary, the question is
"Where do you like it?"

It is a good plan to choose a word with several different meanings, such as box, bill, etc., but usually by the end of the third round it has been guessed. The player from whom he got the clue to the word must then go out while the others choose another object.

No 31
OBSTACLE RACE

*This is a most amusing game and causes plenty of
laughter and enjoyment.*

Those who do not know the game are sent out of the
room and called in one by one. Two or three small objects,
such as a footstool and an ornament or two are placed in a
line on the floor, and the one who is called in is told that
he has to walk blindfolded over these without touching
them. He is blindfolded accordingly, and before he begins
his pilgrimage the objects are quietly removed, so that he
steps very carefully trying to avoid what are not there. Note
the look of disgust on his face when the bandage is removed and he realises that he has been 'done'.

No 32
HOW DO YOU LIKE YOUR NEIGHBOURS?

One of the company stands in the middle of the room
while the others sit round in a circle in which there are no
superfluous chairs. The one standing then asks one or another the question "How do you like your neighbours?"
to which the one asked may reply either "Very much" or

"Not at all". If he likes them very much, everyone in the room must change chairs at once, the one standing trying to get a seat for himself, the player left out taking his place and continuing the questioning. If, however, the answer is "Not at all" he is asked whom he would like to change places with them, and he has to choose two others, who must do their best to change places with his objectionable neighbours, the questioner trying to secure one of their places before the others can sit down, the one left out having next to ask the question.

Whiter than Snow on a Raven's Back

No 33
THROWING THE HANDKERCHIEF

The players all stand round in a ring, with the exception of one in the middle, who has to try to catch the handkerchief which is continually being passed from hand to hand or thrown across from one to another. The person on whom, or owing to whose fault, the handkerchief is captured has to take his turn in the middle in place of the one who has caught it.

No 34
I SHINE

Two of the company retire from the room and choose a word with two or more meanings, or two separate words pronounced the same, one taking one meaning while the other takes the second. They then return, and the first describes the meaning he represents, without giving the word away too openly, and, after he has finished, the second in turn describes his meaning. For instance, suppose the word is 'key' and 'quay'. A will say that he is mineral, of different shapes and sizes, found all over the world etc, and B will say that he, too, is found all over the world, he is mineral, but not so many people can use him as can use A. And so on.

When one of the listeners thinks he has guessed the word, he must say "*I Shine*", and then go on to describe what he thinks the word to be. A and B continue their description till most of the others have guessed.

The following is a short list of words that may be used: Air, Aisle (Isle), Angel, Baize, Balance, Ball, Band, Bank, Banker, Bar, Bark, Bat, Beach (Beech), Bell, Birch, Birth (Berth), Bit, Boa Bore, Boor, Bow, Brown, Butt, Capital, Chord (Cord), Clock, Club, Date, Ensign, Eye.

No 35
CLUMPS

Sides are chosen and group themselves in opposite corners of the room. One member of each side then goes out, and together the two decide on some fairly well-known object, such as for instance, the last plank placed in position on the deck of the Lusitania, or some other equally obvious thing. Having decided on one certain thing, they go back into the room to the others, but each goes to the side from which the other came, A going to B's side and B to A's.

Questions are then fired at them quietly from the members of the group to which they have gone, and they may answer only 'Yes' or 'No', no other words being allowed. As soon as one side has guessed the correct object, the members thereof immediately clap their hands, and claim *both* the players who went out. Two more are then send out, one from each side, and so on, the game proceeding till one side has taken all the members from the other, or until those playing seem tired of it. It will surprise those who have not played at the game before how soon one question leads to another, and how quickly the object can be found out in this way.

No 36
CHARADES

This is always a popular game with guests of all ages.

The players divide into two parties, one of which goes out of the room to choose a word with two or more syllables, which is to be guessed by the other side in due time. The commoner the word the harder it is to guess, and words like 'into', 'upon', are favoured by some players; but it is more sporting to choose a more uncommon word, as then more will depend on the acting.

Having chosen the word, which we will suppose to be 'Seaside' they decide to act a certain scene, one of the players having the duty of bringing in the first half of the word *i.e.* 'Sea', in the course of his chatter and acting. The more original the scene the better. Of course, the word must be brought in in as unostentatious a way as possible, so as not to attract the attention of the other side. When they have done sufficient at the first scene they go out of the room again and decide how to bring in the other part of the word, *i.e. 'Side',* acting another scene as they did the former. Having done this, and thus used separately both syllables of the word, they have next to go through a scene in which they can bring in the whole word 'Seaside'.

When they have done this, and the acting is over, the other side is allowed three guesses in which to find the word.

If possible, the actors should dress up, as it causes much more fun to all concerned, but in a small house, where there is no stock of spare clothes, this is often inconvenient, in which case it is best not to say anything about it.

No 37
DUMB CRAMBO

The players are formed into two sides, one of which goes out of the room, the other remaining inside. Those in the room choose a word which they tell the opposite side rhymes with a certain other one, and the others have to come in and act the various words which they think it is until they find the correct one.

The side in the room, for example, chooses the verb 'To Ring', and tells the opponents that the word they have to find rhymes with 'Bring'. Whereupon the others come in and act 'To Sing', or 'To Spring', or some other word ending with '-ing', till at last they come to the word 'Ring', which is received with cheers instead of with hisses. After that, the other side goes out and has to take its turn at guessing.

No 38
FAMILY COACH

This is an ever-popular game with school-children, boys and girls. The players must sit round the room and each choose some part of the family coach - the wheel, the axle, the whip, the seat, Mrs Brown, her baby, the cat, etc etc.

One of the grown-ups must then tell the tale of Mrs Brown's journey in the coach, and of the accidents that befell them; how one of the wheels came off, the axle broke, the baby cried and so on, making it up as she goes along. At the mention of each specific part, the member who has chosen that part must stand up and turn round. But should the words 'Family Coach' be mentioned, all the players must change their seats. Should any fail to do this, or to answer his cue when his part of the coach is mentioned, he must pay a forfeit.

No 39
MIEW

One of the players must be blindfolded and given a short stick. He is turned round three times, so that he cannot remember exactly where each one is sitting, and then has to point his stick at some one who must 'miew' like a cat, disguising his voice as best he can. The person blindfolded has to guess to whom the voice belongs, and, if the guess is correct, he sits down and the other takes his place.

Another way of playing the game.

'The Cat' kneels at the feet of one of the players, who sit round the room, and gazes up into his or her face, saying 'miew' in the most pathetic voice he can command. The one miewed to has to say "Poor Pussy" without even the ghost of a smile. This is repeated three times. If he smiles, he takes the place of the Cat; if not, the Cat goes to the next player, and tries to make him smile in the same way.

It is always difficult for the rest of the company to keep a solemn face during the performance, but they should try.

No 40
STOOL OF REPENTANCE

One of the players goes out of the room, and during his absence, all the others say something about him which is written down on paper, together with the name of the one who has said it. The remarks need not be complimentary. For instance, one may say he has very nice eyes, while the next says that he is very unpunctual, and a third that he really should learn to turn his toes out more, and so on. When every one has said something about him, he is re-called, and told to sit on a chair or footstool in the middle of the room and guess who has given each reason why he is obliged to sit on the 'Stool of Repentance'.

The remarks are then read out one by one, "Somebody says you have very nice eyes," and if he can guess who the perpetrator is, that one must be the next to go out and suffer. If he cannot guess properly the first time, they are read out again, one guess only at each saying being allowed at a time. It makes more fun to give ridiculous reasons than to limit one's self to personal remarks.

No 41
PINNING ON THE DONKEY'S TAIL

A paper figure of a donkey is pinned or otherwise fastened on to the wall or door of the room, and several detachable tails are cut out beforehand so as to be ready for use when required.

Each player in turn is blindfolded and provided with one of the tails, and told to pin it on to the donkey in the place where the tail ought to go. Turn the blindfolded one round once or twice so as to make him not quite sure where the animal is, and then let him go. He is not allowed to feel along the wall with his hands for the beast, but must pin the tail on without the slightest hesitation. At the laugh which arises, he will pull off the bandage, only to find that he has pinned the tail over one ear, or on the shoulder, or on some other inappropriate spot.

A variation can be effected by having the figure of a man instead of a donkey, and asking the company to give him an eye.

PAPER GAMES

Lists
Making Words out of Words
Telegrams
Syllables
Head, Body, Legs
Book Titles
Consequences
Smudgeography
Outlines
Geography

No 42
LISTS

Each player is provided with a piece of paper and a pencil, and then in turn suggests a subject such as 'Author', 'Town', 'Song', etc, which words are written down as called out one below another. When sufficient words have been called out, or when each player has had a turn, a letter is chosen, and in three minutes, each writes on his paper, opposite the words already written, the name of an author beginning with the letter chosen, a town beginning with the same letter, and so on down the list. When the three minutes are finished, "*Time*" is called and all must stop writing, whether their lists are complete or not.

The players read out their lists, crossing off those that any one else has, and he who has the most names unlike any one else's is declared the winner. It will make the method of play clearer if an example is given. The players in turn call out a subject, as mentioned above, and a letter, say M, is chosen. The list will then read as follows:-

Author	Meredith	
Town	Manchester	
Song	Maud	...... and so on.

No 43
MAKING WORDS OUT OF WORDS

Each player is provided with a pencil and a piece of paper. A long word, containing about ten or a dozen letters, is chosen and written at the top of the paper. Each player must then, in a given time, make as many English words as he can out of this word, using only such letters as are contained in the given word, and not using any letter twice unless it occurs twice originally.

The point of the game is to get as many words as possible out of the original, the one with the greatest number calling out his list first, the others checking it, marking off their own words as they are called out, the one with the greatest number unlike any one else's being counted the winner.

The best way is to take each letter in turn, in order they occur, allowing two minutes to each letter, and reading out each list before going on to the next letter. This makes the game more lively.

Good words to choose are such as the following:
Perambulation, Experimentally, Immeasurable, Mispronunciation, Rejuvenescence, Notwithstanding, Conscientiously, Antediluvian, Constantinople, Enfranchisement.

No 44
TELEGRAMS

This is another quiet paper game. Each player is supplied with a piece of paper and a pencil, and then in turn mentions some letter of the alphabet, which all write down one below the other. When this has been done, they are allowed five minutes in which to make up a telegram, the words of which shall begin with the letters as mentioned in the order given. Thus: the letters as mentioned are, say, M.P.L.D.W.B.A.T.J. One of the telegrams may then read as follows: 'Meet Philip Liverpool Docks Wont Be After Ten John'. At the end of the five minutes, the telegrams are passed along and read out by one of the company.

No 45
SYLLABLES I

Each player is given a piece of paper and a pencil. A word of five or six letters is chosen, and written downwards and upwards in two parallel columns. Say the word chosen is 'STONE'; it is written thus:

S	E
T	N
O	O
N	T
E	S

Each player must then fill in the space between each pair of letters with words of as many syllables as he can find, the words beginning with the first letter and ending with the second, - the more uncommon the word is, the better. The first word, for instance, must begin with S and end with E. At the end of a given time, say three minutes, all must stop writing, and the players, in order, then call out the words they have written. If another has put down the same word as it is called out, both cross it off their lists and do not count any points for it. If, however, no one else has it, then one point is counted for each syllable, the one with the most points at the end of the reading, winning the game.

No 46
SYLLABLES II

This is a variation of the preceding game, and has proved more enjoyable, if not more than a dozen people are playing. If there are more, they are apt to get out of hand.

Sides are chosen, and each player provided with paper and pencil. A word five or six letters is chosen and written downwards and upwards as shown in the last game. Each player must fill in the space between each pair of letters with words which begin with the first and end with the second of the letters (see the preceding game). Proper nouns and foreign words are not allowed. After three or four minutes, all must stop writing, and one of A's side then describes the first word he has written, the others trying to guess what the word is. One minute is allowed for the description, and a further minute for the guessing, no one guessing till the description is finished.

The one who guesses first scores a point for the side to which he belongs. This is followed by one of B's side, and so on alternately, till all the words have been described, and if possible guessed, finishing with one pair of letters before starting with the second. If, however, no one can guess the word within the minute, a point is scored to the side to which the describer belongs. It is as well, to avoid argument, to appoint a time-keeper and scorer before the describing begins.

No 47
HEAD, BODY, LEGS

This is an easy paper game, and popular, especially with the younger members of the party. To each player is given a strip of paper, on which he draws a head of some sort, without telling or showing any one the kind of head he has drawn. He then folds the paper in such a way that nothing but the two lines of the neck are visible. The paper is then passed on to his neighbour, who attaches to the neck some sort of body. The paper is again folded, leaving only the lines for the beginning of the legs, and passed on to the next person, who has to add the legs, though he has no idea what the body is like. The completed drawing is passed on again and then opened, and sent round for all to see. The completed pictures are usually very funny.

No 48
BOOK TITLES

The players are provided with paper and pencils and are asked to draw a picture representing the title of some book. When they have done this, the drawings are passed round, the others writing in turn at the bottom, and folding the paper so that their guesses will not be seen by the rest, what book they think it is meant to represent.

This can be varied by substituting for titles of books, scenes from history etc. This is a very good and amusing game, some of the guesses being very far wrong.

No 49
CONSEQUENCES

Each player is provided with paper and a pencil, and writes at the top of it an adjective suitable for a man. Then folding the paper so that the word cannot be seen, he passes it on to his left-hand neighbour, who writes down the name of a man, real or imaginary. The paper is folded again and passed on to the next one who puts down an adjective suitable for a lady and so on, the paper between each step in the writing being folded and passed on to the left.

The words to be written are as follows:-

An adjective suitable for a gentleman.........
A gentleman's name...................................
An adjective suitable for a lady...................
A lady's name...
Where they met...
What he said to her....................................
What she said to him..................................
What the consequence was.........................
What the world said...................................

When this is complete, the papers are passed on again, and then read out. One or two words have to be understood, and the reading will be something like this: "Bronzed Tom Jones *met* pretty Miss Smith *at* the Marble Arch. *He said to her* 'Chase me girls, I'm a duck.' *She said to him* 'Not really?' *The consequence was* they got married. *And the world said* it served him right."

No 50
SMUDGEOGRAPHY

Half sheets of notepaper are needed. The player writes his full name in ink with a thick pen across the paper, which, while the ink is still wet, is folded down the middle of the writing. When the paper is opened again there is, as a rule, a skeleton or some weird and strange form revealed, which is said to be the skeleton of the owner of the signature. The fun can be increased by asking each one to put clothes on to his skeleton and turn it into a man or woman, as the case may be.

No 51
OUTLINES

This is a very good paper game. Each player puts five dots anywhere on the piece of paper given to him. The papers are then put into the middle of the table, into the pool, and each of the artists draws one out. The players must sketch some figure, view, or object, which touches at some point five dots on the paper. The one who makes the best drawing wins the game.

No 52
GEOGRAPHY

This is another paper game. Each player must in three minutes write down as many geographical names as he can remember, the list being limited to words beginning with a certain letter, which is chosen by chance before the time of starting. At the end of the three minutes, the one with the most names on his list reads his words out, those having the same names on their lists calling out "Yes" and crossing it off, at the same time counting one point for each player who has not got it. When all the lists have been read in turn, the points are added up, the one having the greatest number of names that no one else has, winning the game.

This can be varied by limiting the lists to names of towns or rivers, etc.

NOISY GAMES

Cockfighting
I've been to Paris
Musical Instruments
Knight of the Whistle
Hot Potatoes
Proverbs
Are you there?
Thank you
Priest Cap
Waxworks
Balloons

No 53
COCKFIGHTING

This is for gentlemen only, thought the ladies will enjoy looking on. Two men sit on the floor, hugging their knees with their arms and clasping their hands round their shins. (If necessary, the hands should be tied with a handkerchief; at any rate they must not unclasp them.) Under the knees and above the arms of each man is placed a walking-stick. The men are then placed side by side and told to try to push each other over; the one first succeeding in this attempt, wins, and another pair takes their place.

No 54
I'VE BEEN TO PARIS

The players sit round the room, and the one to the extreme right says to his neighbour, "*I've been to Paris.*" The neighbour must then say "*What did you buy?*" to which the answer from No 1 is "*A pair of scissors*". No 2 goes through the same performance with No 3, and so on round the room. Starting the second round the first sentences are repeated and No 1 says he has bought *a pair of scissors and a fan;* on the third round, *a pair of scissors, a fan and a rocking horse;* some further acquisition at the beginning of each round, which is solemnly repeated by each in turn.

But merely to repeat the words is not all the game. The most amusing part of it is the repeating of the actions, for as each one mentions the various articles which have been purchased in Paris, he must show his neighbour how it works, so that by the end of the game those who have not stopped will be doing several quite different things at the same time, as well as making noises in imitation of the birds and animals. Thus, in the list suggested above, the first one will begin by working his fingers as if he were using scissors. At the second round, besides using the scissors, he will be fanning himself, and at the third he will add rocking himself to his other accomplishments. It is not difficult to imagine what a noise there is when all are trying to do different things at the same time.

No 55
MUSICAL INSTRUMENTS

All the players sit round the room, each choosing a different musical instrument, which he must play in imagination when called upon by the Conductor, who sits in the middle of the circle where he can be easily seen by them all. The Conductor must himself imitate the playing of the instruments, changing quickly from one to another, the bandsman whose instrument he is playing at once following his example, taking up the work and playing for all he is worth till the Conductor changes. Should the instrumentalist fail to take the cue, he must pay a forfeit.

No 57
KNIGHT OF THE WHISTLE

All who do not know this game are asked to leave the room. Each is called back in turn, but only one at once. On entering the room, the novice is presented to the Commander of the Order of the Silver Whistle, and told that if he wishes to become a member of the Order, he must go through a certain ceremonial which is necessary and interesting. In short, he must be blindfolded while one of the Knights hides the insignia of the Order, the Silver Whistle, which he must subsequently find. On finding it, he will be received with open arms.

Having consented to be blindfolded by the Commander, he is led into the centre of the room, where, while the others crowd round him, he is blindfolded and the whistle, which is attached to a short piece of string, is fastened to the back of his coat. The whistle is blown once or twice, just to give him an idea as to which part of the room it has been hidden in, and then the bandage is taken from his eyes and he proceeds to search. Of course, every time he turns round to look for the whistle, which always sounds behind him, another member blows it again, and the novice turns round again. This goes on till he has discovered where the thing is hidden, when he duly becomes a Knight and helps to mystify the next one who is brought in.

This is a capital game for creating plenty of fun, and the laughter and noise coming from the room will only help to whet the appetites of those who are left temporarily outside.

No 57
HOT POTATOES

All the players sit round the room in a circle with the exception of one who stands in the centre. A serviette or handkerchief is then thrown to one of the players, who must immediately throw it to someone else, not waiting even to make it into a better and tighter bundle. The one in the centre tries to catch the serviette as it passes from one to another, and if he succeeds the one from whom it is sent or through whose fault it is secured must take his place in the centre.

No 58
PROVERBS

Two players go out, the rest sitting round the room and choosing a proverb containing the same number of words as there are players left in the room. A well-known tune is then fixed on, and when the two re-enter the room, the others sing their words to the tune, each singing only the one word which has been allotted to him. From the noise thus made the two have to guess the proverb.

A variant of this is that the players, instead of singing their words to a definite tune, must shout them out altogether, so that the noise almost drowns the separate words.

If the number of players left in the room is large, and no proverb can be found long enough, two or more may take the same word. If this be necessary, the two who have to discover the proverb should be told on entering where it starts and where it ends, and that it goes round twice or three times as the case may be.

A variation of this second way of playing the game is for the two discoverers to ask each of the players in turn any question they like, the players having to bring in their special words in their answers. Either way is good, at first perhaps, being the best if the company is a large one.

No 59
ARE YOU THERE?
FOR GENTLEMEN ONLY

A very amusing and quite harmless game

Two gentlemen are blindfolded and lie on their backs on the floor, their feet pointing to opposite corners of the room, their heads about a yard apart. Each is then given a newspaper rolled up. On one asking the question "*Are you there?*" the other answers "*Yes,*" and both then have to strike at where they think the head of the other is. They may, of course, dodge as far as possible, but must not get up from the floor.

No 60
THANK YOU

This is a very good game for teaching children to be polite!

It is played like 'Happy Family'. Each player has an equal number of cards, all the pack being dealt out. The one on the left of the dealer then asks another for a certain card, *e.g.* the four of Hearts; but he must have the four of another suit in his hand or he may not ask for it. Having received the four of Hearts he must say, "*Thank you,*" or he forfeits the card and loses the next turn. If one who has been asked for the card has not got it, he says, "*Not at home*," and has the right to ask for the next card. "*Thank you*" must always be said on receipt of a card.

No 61
PRIEST-CAP

*To be really exciting, this game should be played
as quickly as possible*

All sit round the room and are numbered off from the right, - one, two, three, and so on - each keeping the same number all through the game. The Priest, who sits at one end, then says "*I call upon Number 7*" or whichever number he likes, and Number 7 must answer, "*Not I sir,*" before the Priest can count five. If he fails to do this he must go to the bottom of the line, but if he answers in time, the Priest asks him, "*Who, then?*" to which he must reply some other number, and the number thus called upon must repeat the process. In this game the ladies try to get all the men at the bottom of the row, while the men do their best to send the ladies there. The difficulty lies in remembering the numbers of the others, as, if No 7, in answer to "*Who, then?*" gives the number of the one at the end of the row, he must take the bottom place himself, the rest moving up.

No 62
WAXWORKS

This is very amusing. The players are placed in various positions, and the audience must be on the opposite side of the room. A showman is necessary, someone who is able to talk fluently, as much of the success of the game depends on him.

He describes each waxwork figure in turn, pointing out its various peculiarities, remarking on its beauty and so on, during which time the figure in question must not move a muscle. The showman then lifts the figures to the front of the stage and winds them up, after which they must work their limbs very stiffly for a few seconds and then stop suddenly. The figures may represent any well-known picture or story; as, for instance, the Sleeping Beauty and the Prince, Little Jack Horner, Queen Philippa and the six men of Calais, the Giggling Girl, the more absurd the representation and the costume the better.

This will be found to fill up very pleasantly an odd half-hour at Social Evenings and the like, the actors, of course, being trained beforehand and the showman well-drilled in his speech. When well done, the efforts will be enthusiastically received by the audience.

No 63
BALLOONS

This is a game in which the players are divided into two sides, and seated in two straight rows, four or five feet apart. At an equal distance between the chairs, a tape or string is tightly fixed on the floor. A toy balloon is then thrown up into the air, each side trying to get the balloon on to the floor on the other side of the tape. Should it fall on their own side of the tape, one goal is counted to their opponents, but if on the other, they score the goal. The players *must remain seated*, and hit the balloon with *the back of the right hand only*. The side against whom the goal is scored has the privilege of 'Kicking off,' *i.e.* throwing up the ball to start again.

The game continues until one side has scored thirteen goals (or any number that has been decided on beforehand).

N.B. – It is advisable to have two or three balloons in reserve.

The Game of Cities

S.T. 207.

**Afternoon
Tea Games.**

12 in. Box, with
Key, amusing and
instructive. The
following games at
1/1 per box :—

QUIET GAMES

Missing Adjectives
The Seven Blows of Circumstance
Co-operative story telling
Notable Men
Impromptu Speeches
Shakespeare's Characters
Man and his Object

No 64
ADJECTIVES

Sides are chosen, one side choosing an adjective with the same number of letters as there are players on that side, for instance the word 'Tight' may be chosen if there are five players on the side. Then each of the party takes one of the letters and finds an adjective beginning with that letter, No 1 taking T, No 2 taking I, and choosing words like 'Tired' and 'Idle' to represent their letters. Each of the five then acts his adjective. Tired, Idle, Gentle, etc, and the opponents have first to find out what each is representing, and then what the whole word is. When the word has been guessed, the other side chooses another adjective, and so on.

No 65
MISSING ADJECTIVES II

This is a variation of Number 27, but more amusing, and requires similar preparations. Take a somewhat longer paragraph from some novel, - sensational if possible, - and make a list of the adjectives contained therein, writing each on a separate slip of paper. These slips are then shuffled and dealt round till all are given out. Then start to read out the paragraph, omitting the adjectives, which are supplied as required by each player in turn reading out the adjective on the top of the pile dealt out to him. As can be imagined, the result is not always what might be expected.

No 66
THE SEVEN BLOWS OF CIRCUMSTANCES
A CARD GAME

The 1,2,3,4,5,6,7 of Hearts are taken from a pack of cards and put in a ring on the table. These are the Seven Blows of Circumstances, and the pool is the centre of it. A card from the rest of the pack is dealt out to each player, and also a tiny slip of paper on which is written the player's name, so that each player has his own name on the slip. The object and hope of each player is to get a low-numbered card (the Ace counting as the lowest), as the player with the highest card has to put on a 'blow', *i.e.* place his square of paper on the Ace of Hearts, and every time his card is the highest he has to move it on to the next, until after the seventh he is submerged in the pool and out of the game. Then he can only return into the game by getting somebody to speak to him. Whoever forgets sufficiently to speak to him puts on a blow, and from the pool the other is raised to the seventh, so that he has another 'life' left.

The first player to whom the cards have been dealt has the option of passing his card, if it be a high one, to his left-hand neighbour and receiving his in exchange. At this time, he must not look (under penalty of adding a blow to his account) until each of the other players has changed or refused to change according to his wish. The second player looks at the card dealt to him, or the one handed on by his neighbour, No 1, and if he thinks it too high, he can pass it on in his turn and take that of No 3. This goes on till all but the last dealt to has passed on or changed; he may take a card at random from the pack, if he wishes. Then at last all the cards are turned face upwards, and the one with the highest card has to take unto himself a blow. The game goes on until all but one are in the pool, and causes plenty of fun, especially when several of the players have taken on six or seven blows of circumstances.

No 67
CO-OPERATIVE STORY-TELLING

This is quite simple, though not so easy to do as it seems at first sight. The players sit round the room and one begins to tell a tale. At the end of one minute his left-hand neighbour takes it up where he left it, continuing the story for another minute, and so on, each being allowed one minute only. The story can last any length of time, but it should be the object of each succeeding raconteur to make the plot more complicated for those who follow, till it comes to the last round, when every one tries to account successfully for and put out of the story at least one of the characters. Much fun can be got by introducing references to events of the day.

No 68
NOTABLE MEN

This is a game in which any number can play. Two of the company go out of the room; the rest choose some celebrity whose name contains the same number of letters as there are players left in the room. Say there are eleven players seated round the room; they choose, for example, the name 'Shakespeare'. Each one in turn then takes a letter, the first taking S, the second H, and so on. Each player then decides, without consulting the others, on some well-known character whose name begins with his letter. Thus the first may take Samuel, the second Henry VIII, the third Alfred, and so on. The two from outside are then called in and listen while the others in turn describe their heroes. If the descriptions are good, it is sometimes necessary for the listeners to ask for them to be repeated and continued later on in the game, after they have heard what the others have to say. Their work is to guess, first the names of the well-known characters, Samuel, Henry, etc, and from them the name of the celebrity.

No 69
IMPROMPTU SPEECHES

Each player writes a subject, humorous or otherwise, on a slip of paper, which he puts into a hat. In another hat are papers containing the names of the people present. Then a paper is drawn from the second hat, and the person named thereon is told to speak for five minutes on a subject drawn from the other hat. Until the five minutes are over, the speaker may not resume his seat, even though he has nothing to say.

A more interesting way of playing this is as follows: One of the party gets up and makes a speech, or rather some remark, on any subject whatever, and at every stop the rest of the company is obliged to call out "Hear, Hear!" If any one forgets or misses, he must stand up and make a speech instead of the original orator. The fun consists in saying things to which every one cannot agree, and so catching them.

No 70
SHAKESPEARE'S CHARACTERS

*This is a good memory game
for a fairly well-educated gathering*

Papers and pencils are necessary, and then those present are given five minutes or so in which to write down as many of the characters in the plays of Shakespeare (or, if preferred, the names of the plays themselves instead) as each can remember. When "Time" is called, the players in turn read out their lists, marking off those that others have, and counting those that no one else has.

(A variation in the way of counting in these games is to count one point for each member who has not got the word. Thus, with nine players, and three others having the word, the one who is reading out his list will put down 5, – not 6, as he himself has it.)

No 71
MAN AND HIS OBJECT

Two persons leave the room, and choose a well-known man (living or dead) and some characteristic of his, as, for instance, King Alfred and the Cakes, or Nero and his Fiddle. They then return to the room, and one impersonates the man while the other takes the object, each in turn describing what he stands for, till two of the listeners have guessed. The two first to find out what they represent go out the next time.

This can be varied by the members of the company asking questions of the man and his object, and discovering for themselves what they represent.

TABLE GAMES

Table Bowls
"Up Jenkins!"
Advertisement Snap
Grab Cork
Drawing through a Mirror
Mixed Letters
Drawing a watch from memory
Butterflies

No 72
TABLE BOWLS

The players are divided into two sides, and, provided with two Draughts each, sit on opposite sides of the table, from which the cloth has been removed. Then one player flips with his finger one of his Draughts, trying to get it as near the centre of the table (marked by a piece of stamp-paper) as he can. He is followed by one of the other side, who tries to knock the other Draught away or leave his own nearer the centre that the other. Another of the first side then follows, and so on alternately, till all have sent their two pieces each. The side which has the piece nearest the centre counts one point, and an additional point is counted for every additional one nearer than any belonging to the other side. Thus, if there are three whites nearer the centre than the nearest black, then the whites count three points, and not merely one for having the nearest.

It is as well to decide beforehand how many points make the game. Thirteen is a good number.

No 73
"UP, JENKINS!"

This is a very good game for not more than twelve people. Six sit on each side of the table, from which the cloth has been removed. A captain is appointed for each side, and if a player obeys the orders of any but the captain of his or the other side, his side forfeits the point.

A sixpence is the only thing necessary for the game. A's side takes it first and, with the hands under the table, so that the coin can pass from one to another without being seen by the opponents, one of the party secretes it in the palm of the hand, in such a way that when the hand is on the table the others cannot tell where the coin is. B, the captain of the other side, then orders them to put their hands on the table. This can be done in two ways - with a bang, in which case they must bang their hands on the table (usually making as much noise as possible to drown any possible clink of the sixpence) or with a creep, when the hands are put down on to the table gently and opened slowly, the palms, of course, always being downwards. B's side next consults as to where the coin is, judging by the look of the hands. First this and then that hand is decided against, and the owner told by captain B to take it off, till only one remains on the table. Should they make a mistake, however, and say "*Up Jenkins!*" to the hand in which the treasure is, the coin is shown immediately, and the point goes to A's side, who again hides the sixpence. If B has guessed right, and it has not come to light before the last hand is left on the table, the point goes to B, and the coin is passed over to him, and his party hides it in the same way. The side that scores thirteen points first, wins the game.

No 74
ADVERTISEMENT SNAP

This is played like ordinary snap, *i.e.* the cards are dealt round, and each player in turn plays a card, without having previously seen it, face upwards on the table. It differs from ordinary snap, however, in that each player before starting the game must choose some well-known advertisement, the longer the better, which has to be remembered by all the others.

When two of the players have put down similar cards, say two Queens, instead of shouting "Snap", each must shout out the advertisement chosen by the other, the one finishing first getting both heaps of cards. It will be seen that the longer the advertisement the better the game and the less chance the player has of losing his cards.

No 75
GRAB CORK

This is played like ordinary snap, but when two cards are alike, instead of shouting "Snap" the two owners must seize a cork that is in the middle of the table. The one who manages the get the cork then takes both sets of cards.

No 76
DRAWING THROUGH A MIRROR

Each of the players should be asked in turn to draw a pig, or other object, on a paper, while looking through a mirror and not directly on to the paper. It is much harder than it seems.

A more difficult object to draw is a watch, the players being asked to make the fingers pointing to a definite time.

No 77
MIXED LETTERS

Printed letters of the alphabet are sold at toyshops, and these are necessary for this game, which is very good for children of all ages who have a wet half-hour to spend. The letters are divided equally among those who are playing, and turned face downwards on the table. The first player then turns a letter face upwards, the others in turn following suit. Should A have in his row of letters that are turned up sufficient to make a word, he places them, in the right order of the word they spell, in front of him. Should B have in his row others that with A's word will make a longer one, he may take those of A, who can only win them back by making a still longer word with them and some additional ones. This game goes on till all the letters are used, and is quite enjoyable. Of course B can take from any of the other players, and not only from those next to him.

No 78
DRAWING A WATCH FROM MEMORY

Give the would-be artists paper and pencils and then hold up a watch, face forward, for half a minute, during which time they must do nothing but look at it. At the end of that time, take it away and tell them to draw the face of the watch. This appears to be easy, but there are one or two points which are overlooked frequently, and it is surprising how often the small things escape notice. For instance, the number four, is it IIII or IV? Are the seconds shown? How much of the six and seven can be seen? etc.

No 79
BUTTERFLIES
A brush game

Three small pots of paint, of different colours, (*e.g.* red, yellow and blue), and a small brush must be procured beforehand. Each player takes a clean sheet of notepaper, and, having written his name on the back, puts two dots of paint, choosing which two of the three colours he likes, one just above the other in the middle of the sheet. This he doubles down the middle and presses outwards, with a flat knife, in the shape of a butterfly's wings. The paper is then opened, and with a pen and ink feelers are added. The best butterfly wins the prize, if there be one.

TRICKS ETC

Which hand did I lift up?
Sitting on Bottles
Magic Counting
Good Old Port
Balancing in a Clothes Basket
Magic Writing
Thought Reading
Blowing out the Candle
Balancing a bottle on the head
Picking up a cork with the mouth

No 80
WHICH HAND DID I LIFT UP?
This is a puzzle, but a very good one.

Two players must know it, one to go out and guess, the other to stay in and perform. The one in the room places both his hands on his knees, then lifts one up while he counts ten, professedly to give the others a good chance to look at the hand and then he puts it back again on his knee. The accomplice then comes in and tells him which hand he lifted up. After this has been done two or three times some of the others will think they know and volunteer to go out, but they will be unable to guess right each time unless they have really found out how it is done. Encourage them to try: it makes the thing look more difficult and wonderful.

The point of the whole thing is that the blood rushes down to the hands when they are resting on the knees, but when one is held up in the air above the head while ten is being counted, the blood rushes back again. If the accomplice returns quickly enough he sees the hand back in position but free from the full veins which tell the tale.

No 81
SITTING ON BOTTLES

This is for gentlemen only to do, but very amusing for the ladies who are watching.

Two empty wine bottles are provided, and on each a man must sit and balance himself, raising his feet from the floor, and not supporting himself in any way with his hands. To one is then given a lighted taper, and to the other an unused one. Then the one with the unused taper has to try to light it from the lighted one which the other balancer is holding.

(N.B. – An unused taper is harder to light than one which has already been used.)

No 82
MAGIC COUNTING

The only necessaries for this simple game are two confederates and three walking sticks. One of the confederates goes out of the room, while the other asks the company to choose a number not higher than 999. A number having been chosen, for instance 835, he proceeds, with much hard thinking, to arrange the sticks on the floor so that his friend will recognise the number when he returns.

The explanation is this: the lowest stick represents units, the middle one tens, and the top one hundreds, and they are so placed that the lowest shall point to five o'clock, the middle one to three o'clock, and the top one to eight o'clock of an imaginary clock face, the twelve o'clock of which must always be nearest the fireplace. Ten, eleven and twelve o'clock stand for 0, for obvious reasons.

No 83
GOOD OLD PORT

This is not quite so easy as it seems at first sight. Paper and pencil are given to all who wish to try – and all should – then the hostess reads out the following letters, telling her guests to write them down one after another without any stops or spaces: GDLDPRTFRRTHDXXFRDDNS.

The guests are to make a sentence out of these letters by putting in wherever and as often as they wish, one vowel and one vowel only. The missing vowel, which they are not told till they have tried properly, is O, and when placed in its right position, the sentence reads thus: "Good old port for orthodox Oxford dons."

No 84
BALANCING IN A CLOTHES-BASKET
This is not quite as easy as it sounds. Try it!

A clothes basket is balanced, by means of its handles, on a stout pole, which is resting on two chairs. On one of the chairs is placed an apple. With his back to this apple, one of the gentlemen, already provided with a walking stick, attempts to enter the basket, balance himself therein, and then with the stick knock the apple at his back off the chair.

No 85
MAGIC WRITING

One who knows the trick goes out of the room, while his confederate, provided with a walking-stick, asks the company to choose some word of not too many letters. A is then called back into the room and B proceeds to make with the stick several hieroglyphic, meaningless signs in a careful way, so as to deceive as far as possible the lookers-on, punctuating the signs with short sentences having no apparent relation or reference to the word chosen, and which, he explains beforehand, or, if he can work it in, during the performance, are but to pass the time. But really each sentence must begin with a letter of the chosen word, and it is from these that the reader of the magic writing gets the consonants. The vowels are indicated by giving, for A one thump with the stick on the floor, for E two thumps, for I three thumps, for O four and for U five.

Take the word 'Stamp' for example. After a few mysterious tracings on the floor the writer will say to the other, "Stand a little farther this way, please," and continue writing all the time. "Take that chair won't you?" he will then add and then give one thump on the floor for the vowel A. 'M' comes next and so he says, "Mind! you are in the way there," and after some more writing he finishes up by saying, "Please tell me what the word is now," and he has spelt 'STAMP'.

It will be found usually that there are several clever people in the room who are quite certain that they have discovered how it is done. Let them try.

No 86
THOUGHT READING

The player who leaves the room must have a confederate, and they must agree on some sign which the confederate can give as a signal when touching the object chosen. For instance, it might be the third object pointed at after something black, or instead of saying, "Is it this?" he might say, "Is it that?" and the chosen object be the second thing pointed at after the word 'that'. Any of the company chooses the object after the player has left the room. When he comes back his confederate points to different things saying all in the same tone of voice, "Is it this, is it this?" until he points to something black, and the third object after that is the correct one. This game can be made very mystifying, and is usually well-liked between the more lively games.

No 87
BLOWING OUT THE CANDLE

A lighted candle is placed on a table or on the mantel-piece, so that it is about on a level with the head of the average player. One of the company standing three or four yards away from the candle is then blindfolded, and, after having been turned round three times so that he will lose his bearings, is told to go and blow out the light. Of course he must not be able to see through the bandage. The careful way he will step towards the spot where he thinks the candle is, and the wild efforts he makes to blow out the flame, which is often some distance away, will cause no end of amusement. Each of the company in turn should be made to go through the same performance.

No 88
BALANCING A BOTTLE ON THE HEAD

This is a very difficult balancing feat, but one well worth trying. Get a large bottle (empty) and balance it on the back of the head. Then from an upright position get down on the hands and knees, and with the mouth pick up a cork already placed on the floor. Having done this, get up again to the original standing position, remove the bottle from the head and the cork from the mouth, and - acknowledge the applause.

No 89
PICKING UP A CORK WITH THE MOUTH

Place a cork about five feet away from the feet. Lower yourself leaning on one hand, not touching the ground with the other but keeping it on the hip, and pick up the cork with the mouth. Then raise yourself on to your feet again, still using only the one hand. This is not quite so easy as it sounds.

ALPHABETICAL INDEX

ALPHABETICAL INDEX

ALPHABETICAL INDEX

ALPHABETICAL INDEX

ALPHABETICAL INDEX

Other Copper Beech Gift Books to collect:-

HOW TO ENTERTAIN YOUR GUESTS
**A 1911 collection of indoor games
A companion book to 'The Duties of Servants'**

THE LADY'S DRESSING ROOM
**Open the door to beauty and relaxation secrets
from days gone by. How to get up, fresh, beau-
tiful and in an amiable frame of mind with all
your wrinkles smoothed over - and other
fragrant tips from a golden age!**

SOCIAL SUCCESS
**The modern girl's guide to confidence, poise,
manners and tact.
1930s etiquette for all occasions.**

THE SERVANTLESS HOUSEHOLD
**How to cope - some polite advice
Keep the house in order without the benefit
of staff. Maintain high standards and be
prepared for anything!**

THE ETIQUETTE COLLECTION

Etiquette for ~
CHOCOLATE LOVERS
COFFEE LOVERS
THE CHILDREN
THE CHAUFFEUR
DRESS
AN ENGLISH TEA
GENTLEMEN
LOVE & COURTSHIP
MOTORING
NAMING THE BABY
POLITENESS
ENGLISH PUDDINGS
A TRADITIONAL CHRISTMAS
THE TRAVELLER
THE WELL DRESSED MAN
WINE LOVERS

~ good manners for every occasion!
For your free catalogue containing these and other titles write to:

Copper Beech Publishing Ltd
P O Box 159 East Grinstead
Sussex England RH19 4FS
www.copperbeechpublishing.co.uk

ɔ 127 ɔ

www.copperbeechpublishing.co.uk